Kelly & Kim

Have a good [time]

Love,
A.J.

# Teachers! Teachers! Teachers!

## A CARTOON COLLECTION

Edited by
**S. Gross**

**CB**

CONTEMPORARY
BOOKS

A TRIBUNE NEW MEDIA COMPANY

**Library of Congress Cataloging-in-Publication Data**

Teachers! Teachers! Teachers! : a cartoon collection / edited by
S. Gross.
     p.   cm.
  ISBN 0-8092-3347-9
  1. Teachers—Caricatures and cartoons. 2. American wit and humor
Pictorial.  I. Gross, S. (Sam).
NC1426.T43   1995
741.5'973—dc20                            95-35781
                                                    CIP

Cartoons copyrighted by *The New Yorker* are indicated
throughout the book.

Published by Contemporary Books, Inc.
Two Prudential Plaza, Chicago, Illinois 60601-6790
Manufactured in the United States of America
International Standard Book Number: 0-8092-3347-9
10   9   8   7   6   5   4   3   2   1

*To Sarita Abrahams—naturally, a teacher!*

RANDY FREDNER

1

*"This is a student I had back in 1970 B.C. Before computers."*

*"I hope you'll forgive me for being a little nervous this evening. As a teacher I'm not used to talking to so many people who are paying attention."*

3

4

"... and so, remember that # goes with [ ] before %, except after $."

5

*"Our mid-term math test! That's the last time I trick or treat at our teacher's house."*

*"Well, somebody better wake her up. It's past time to go home."*

7

*"Do you realize that you are the first in a thousand generations of your family to attend pre-kindergarten?"*

"Send us anywhere! We're not afraid of terrorists. . . .
We're schoolteachers."

9

*"It's too bad we have to lay off teachers, but who else could we spare?"*

"I prefer to teach at an elementary school.
It's easier to find a parking place."

11

*"In order to cut down disruption in my class I've asked my students not to wear any gang, club, team, or group colors, insignias, patches, etc."*

*"That's the closet, Stuart!"*

13

"*The following schools are closed due to education reform. . . .*"

*"Wait a minute! If I had six Fig Newtons and I gave one to Phyllis and two to Earl . . . why do I only have one left!?!"*

15

"They must be from the school chancellor's office—
they're here in triplicate."

16

*"You will like Mr. Woofard. He has an attention-deficit disorder."*

17

18

" . . . and that's how you kill bison."

# She's been teaching too long!

SIPRESS

*"I'm sorry we couldn't have phoned you earlier to sub today."*

21

S.GROSS

22

"Oh, yes, Billy, you can go home now.
I'm sorry I forgot that I had told you to stay after school."

23

"It's an ad from a new consulting service.
They translate federal guidelines into English."

26

*"Fine thanks I get for teaching you how to write back in second grade!"*

*"You mean you're on sabbatical, too?"*

*"I'm no monster: I'm tough, but I'm fair."*

29

*"This one plays 'Good morning, dear Teacher,' and this one plays
'School days, school days,' and this one plays 'School's out!
School's out! Teacher wore her bloomers out!'"*

*"It's been a typical day for me. I had four students with stomachaches, five students with headaches, and six teachers with shot nerves."*

31

WILLIAM DEWITT
1918 1984

STUDENT
STUDENT-TEACHER
TEACHER

S.GROSS

*"So often you learn why the child has problems as soon as you meet the parents. . . ."*

33

34

"If we run into one of my students, I'll have to stop being normal and act like a teacher for a minute."

35

*"I'll answer any questions except to whom we give thanks."*

*"Hard-disk conversion, 600 dpi scanning, laser printer upgrading . . .
the three R's certainly have changed."*

# TEACHER CALENDAR BAR GRAPH

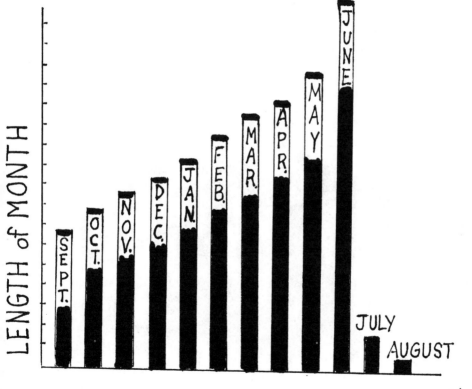

LENGTH of MONTH

SEPT. OCT. NOV. DEC. JAN. FEB. MAR. APR. MAY JUNE JULY AUGUST

Wilkie

39

"You have reached Miss Pemberton. If you want to know the math assignment
for tonight, press one. If you want to know which days I have gym, press two.
If you want the third-period reading list, press three. If you want . . ."

40

*"Despite it being an inner-city school, I understand that it has an outstanding science program."*

41

*"How can he say 'We'll go into that later' when I'm already dying of boredom?"*

43

**★** Answers in back

*"Welcome to James's school, Mrs. Whistler. I recognize you
from his drawing."*

*"Are you chewing gum?"*

*"Knowledge is the ultimate weapon. Next!"*

47

*"I'm mainly interested in something that won't show up
on teaching evaluations."*

"It's the annual elementary school play."

*"Hey, Mister Taxpayer! Thanks for everything!"*

*"Your request to go back to teach in an inner-city school can mean only one of two things: either you are now sufficiently enlightened or the air is too thin for you up here."*

51

*"I think it's called team teaching."*

TEACHER BURN-OUT

1

2

3

4   SCOTY

"In sex education, everyone got incompletes."

*"All right . . . people . . . all right . . .
this faculty meeting will now come to order."*

*"I think that's right, but let me check."*

*"Sorry I'm late. . . . I had to finish correcting some papers."*

THE KNOWLEDGE HUT ®

FORMERLY P.S. 102

58

*"Number three is Mr. Hugo, our seventh grade teacher—the one whose exam contained questions not covered in the assigned reading."*

*"I'll have number four, 'None of the Above.'"*

"Before you removed the mobile classroom,
did you remove the students?"

61

*"Why don't you all put your heads down and cover your little ears while I fix this . . . this . . . blasted projector?"*

62

*"You have many more years of tyrannizing the teaching staff in you."*

© 1990 The New Yorker Magazine, Inc.

*"Well, for starters, Matt has been showing definite improvement in risk-taking."*

"An A student said that to you?"

*"I'm just filing a grievance."*

67

*"I'm trying to get in on one of those lucrative defense contracts . . .
but it's hard when our school only goes up to the sixth grade."*

# CLASSROOM OVERCROWDING SOLVED!

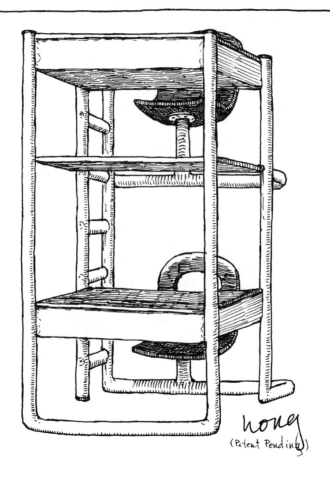

noue
(Patent Pending)

*"I hate when 'messy play' spins out of control."*

# NON-CONTROVERSIAL TEXTBOOKS

"I'm only in my second year of teacher's college
and I'm already feeling burnt-out."

73

*"Everyone gets a passing grade except Jimmy Thorson. . . .
Where is Jimmy, anyway?"*

"Now they're complaining that the surroundings are so beautiful,
they can't keep their minds on their work."

"My husband and I expect you to raise our son with decent values!"

*"Due to budget cutbacks, this year's graduating seniors will each receive one of these lovely handmade diplomas created by Mrs. Murphy's second grade art class."*

*"It is our hope that those of you children who are armed belong to a well-regulated militia."*

79

*"I'm taking a year off to tackle motherhood."*

"I know this school doesn't have a dress code, but for goodness' sake, you're a teacher!"

*"Remember, Miss Martin, when I was a kid in your third grade class and I told you I loved you and when I grew up I was going to marry you? Well . . ."*

*"Today we shall paint a rainbow. The colors available to us are black, yellow, and purple."*

ASBESTOS

A. BACALL

"My third grade boys and I got separated. . . .
Could you direct me to the nudes?"

"I'm afraid of my teacher, my teacher is afraid of the principal, the principal is afraid of the superintendent, the superintendent is afraid of the board of education, and the board of education is afraid of the politicians. . . . What a heck of a way to get an education!"

*"I'm his teacher at P.S. 42. Put him into parochial school."*

*"Teach."*

*"When you grow up—take my word for it—you'll remember me!"*

# Index of Artists